C000090952

KOROMO

All leaves on a tree at first glance seem to be the same but a closer look reveals their difference. Wouldn't it be nice if fabrics produced for clothing could have the same seemingly effortless variety, randomness and

irregularity once more;
Unfortunately modern
production methods
work against this.

Most factories,
machinery and
people are geared
to produce textiles
that are uniform
in weave and
pattern and show

little variance from
one meter of fabric
to the next.
To choose techniques
that are not fully
controllable, to find
the weakness of the
machine to use repeats
that are bigger
than the field of
vision or just

to cheat the unsus-
pecting eye are
some ways of breaking
this tedium.

The biggest luxury,
and the easiest way
to avoid repetiti-
veness is to make
things entirely by
hand.

The fabrics chosen

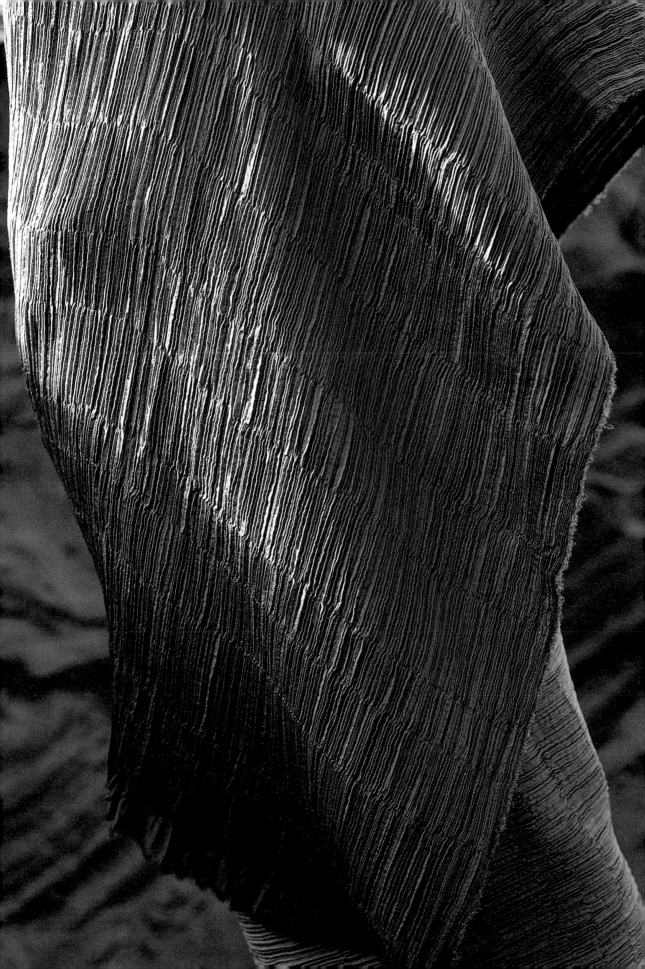

for this book are
all patterned or
have some kind of
visible surface effect,
because, however nice
they might be to wear
plain and solid
colour textiles are
not very photogenic
They were made in
Japan, India, Indonesia

12

China and Korea
because people there
offered patience, skill
and understanding.
The inspiration
came from looking
at nature with
insatiable eyes,
experimenting with
the office tools.
day-dreaming and

a wish to hide the limitations of the techniques used when making fabrics.

The choice of colour is arbitrary, frivolous, sometimes prejudiced and therefore not easy.

[20] The materials are made from natural fibres because these

feel so good and
hopefully give the
wearer a sensation
of comfort, well-
being and pleasure

Jürgen Lehl

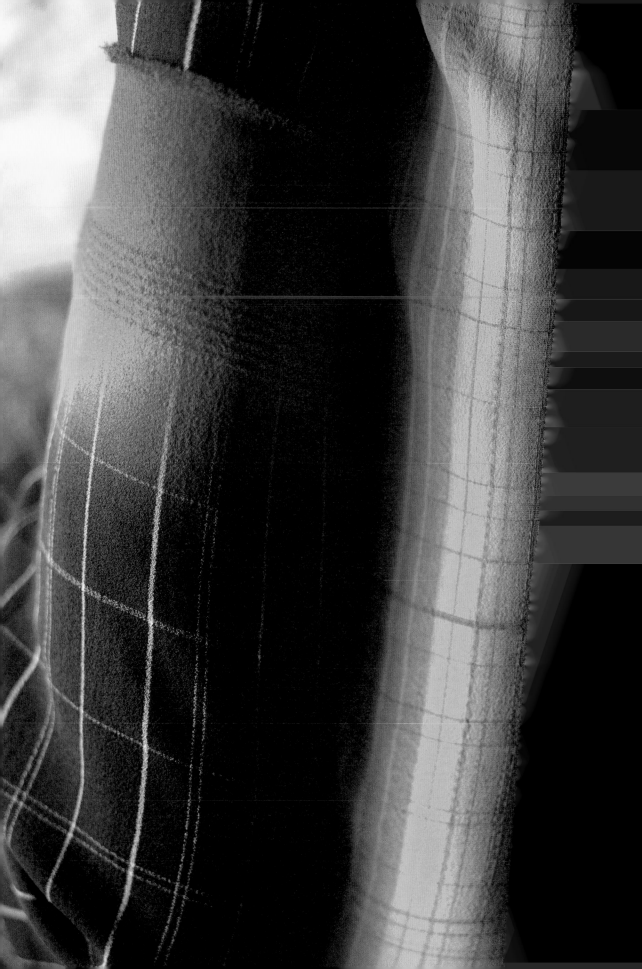

28

40

44

KP

56

60

64

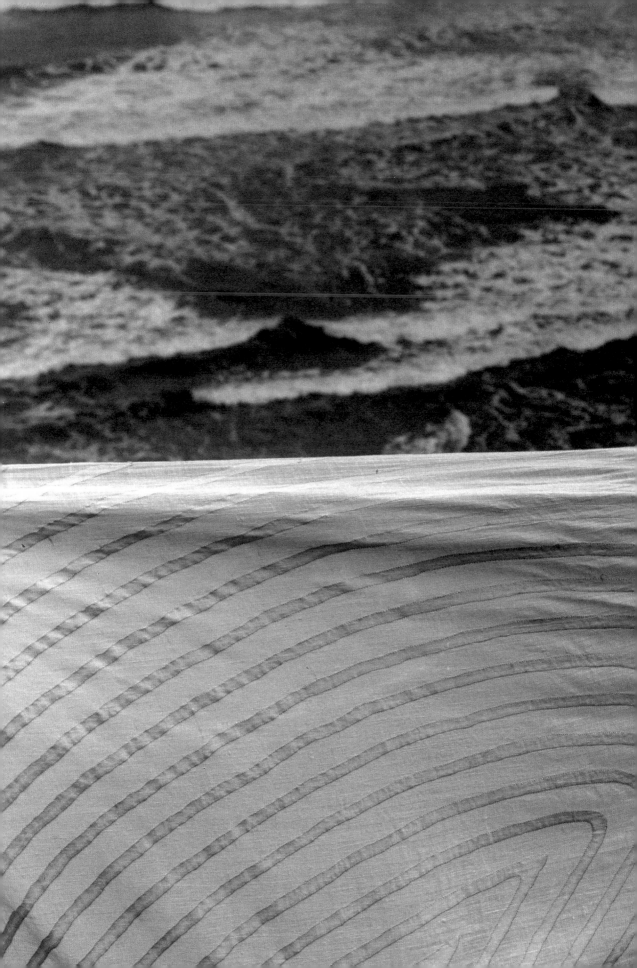

82

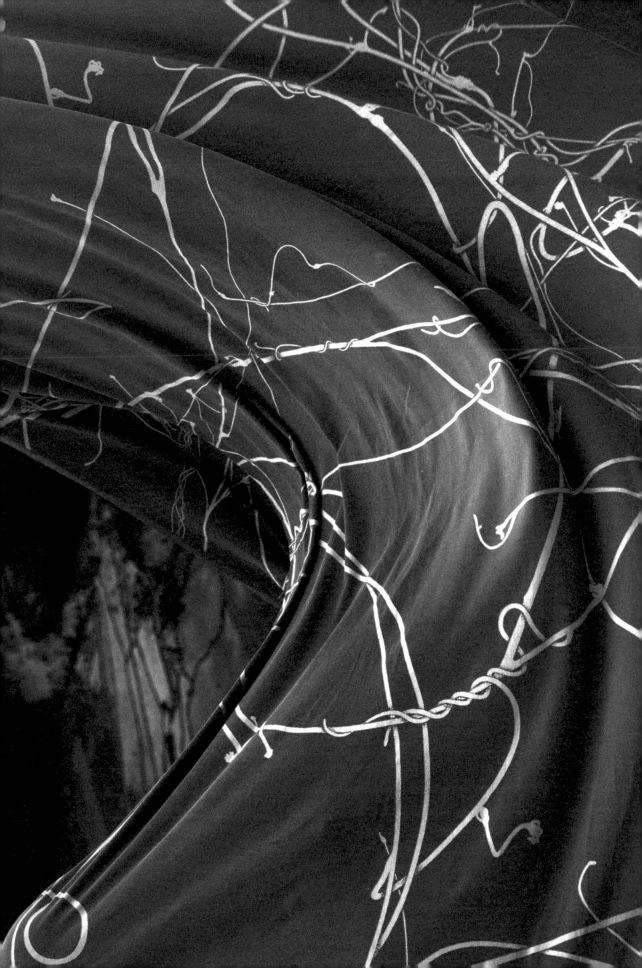

88

92

104

106

110

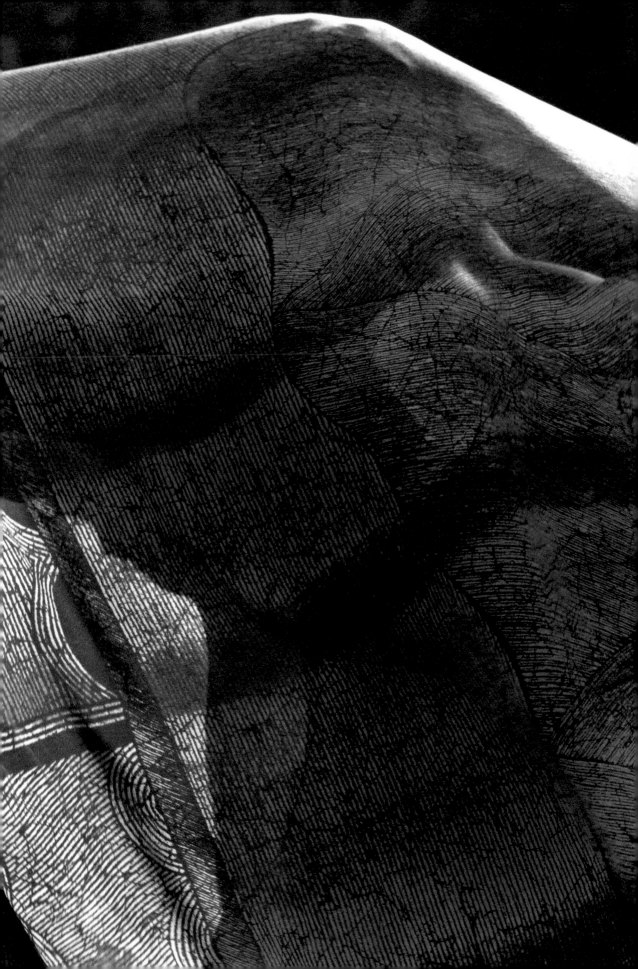

114

118

/22

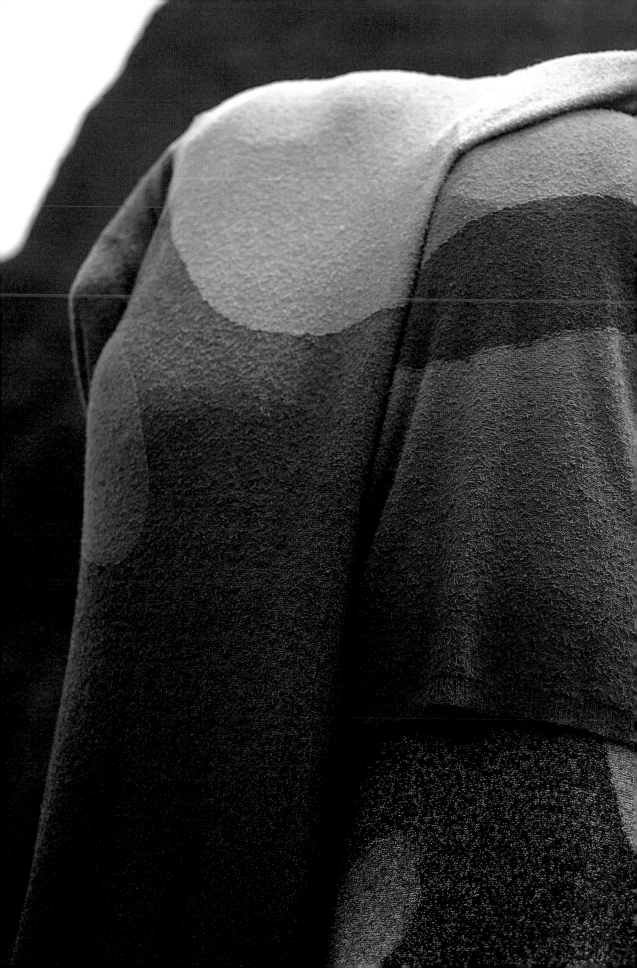

使ってあげますよ

肌ざわりがいいし着る人に

とってはいい心地良く満足や感を

快感をあたえてくれると思う

かうです

よーがくしーV

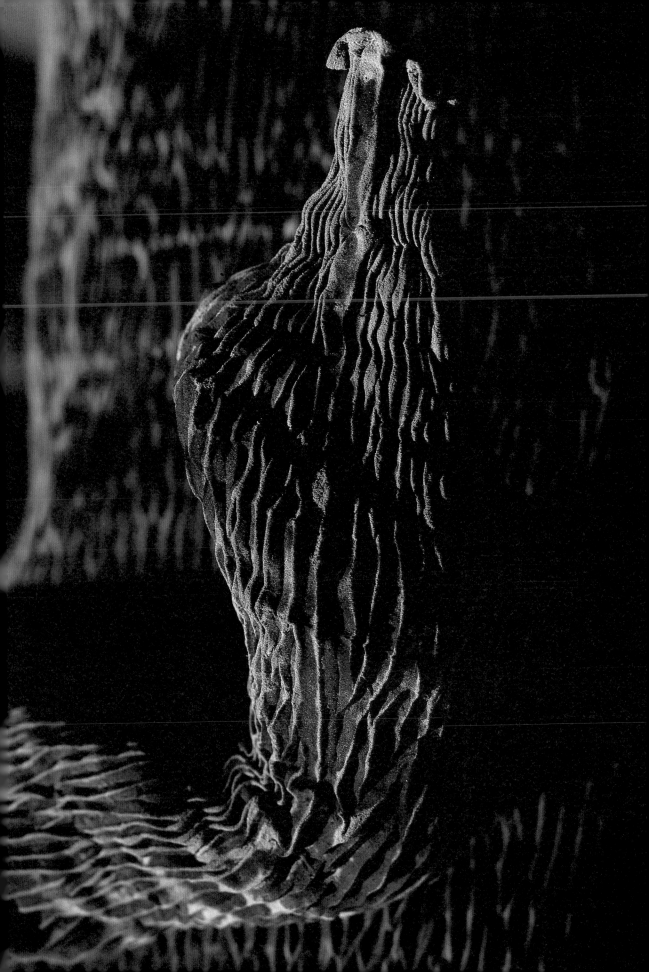

実際に布を作る時に用いら
れる技術の限界を隠したいと
願う気持ちでいます。色を選ぶ
ということは自分勝手で気まま
ぐれで時をして好き嫌いで決まる
ので容易ではよりません
素材は天然自然の繊維を

なんで作られましたというこうした国は

今は忍耐と技と理解と提供

してくれるからです。

言うなれば飽くことを知らない

目で自然を眺めることを手近に

ある道具いで試しに作ってみること

ぼうっと夢想することと、そうして

えるかどうかの表面効果のある
もればかりじゃよ、その沢は月に
もうここに感じなくても
無代・単色のラマックけ
写真に撮るとあまりよく見えな
いようです。これらの布は日本
イ...ネーア・中国・韓国

これが先に述べた退屈をもたらす
破る方法かもしれません 付より
の贅沢はそして一単調な繰り
返しを避けて一番簡単な道は
モノを徹頭徹尾手で作ること
です。一つのモノのために選んだ
はすべて柄織りだった一目に見ん

私の布をもう私の布はほど
んど違いがありませんでして
ってりんのきなことこのある
技術を選ぶ機械の弱さを利
用して視野に納まりきそな
る後を作り出したり純気なく
見るへの目をくらますうな

不揃いを取り戻せたら素敵ではないでしょうか。残念ながら現代は生産方式ではこういうことは正反対の働きをしています。大抵の工場や機械や人間は織り方も柄も画一的なテキスタイルを生み出すように装備されている

ひと目見ただけでは
葉はみな同じに見えます
けれどよく見れば一葉一葉
が違うことが分かってくる
夜服のために作られる体を
それも同じようにいま一度だく
おぜる多様さやばらつきについて